Poptropica English

PUPIL'S BOOK 1

Contents

Welcome

 **1** Listen and point. Then trace.   **2** Listen and chant.

AMAZING HELPER AWARD

1 Charlie

2 Rose

3 Ola

4 Uncle Dan

 3 Listen and point. Then match.

 1 yellow   2 red

 3 green   4 blue

5 orange   

 7 purple   6 pink

     Can say greetings and colours

4 🎧 1:05 **Listen and chant.**

1 2 3 4 5
6 7 8 9 10

5 🎧 1:06 **Look. Listen and sing.**

   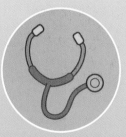

1 My toys

1 ⭐ What do you know?

TOYS

car

boat

bike

doll

£

train

2 🎧 1:07 Listen and circle.

3 🎧 1:08 Listen and say.

Can identify toys

4 🎧 1:09 **Listen and chant.**

kite

ball

5 🎧 1:10 ✏️ **Listen and colour. Then say.**

1 2 3 4 5

What's this?

It's a ball.
It's orange.

6 1:13 **Listen and point. Then say.**

| eleven | twelve | thirteen | fourteen | fifteen |

| sixteen | seventeen | eighteen | nineteen | twenty |

7 1:14 / 1:15 **Listen and find. Then sing.**

  8 1:16 **Listen and say. Then ask and answer.**

How many dolls?

Eleven dolls.

Can use numbers 11–20 / Can sing a song

9   **Say and colour.**
Then play Bingo.

It's a car.
It's red.

SOUNDS FUN!

10 1:17 **Listen and say.**

A hen with a red pen.

A doll in a box with a frog.

12   Act out the story.

Can understand a simple story / Can act out a story

13 Look and write.

1	2	3	4	5	6	7	8		10
11		13		15		17	18		20

14 1:21 Listen and stick. Then say.

Stick

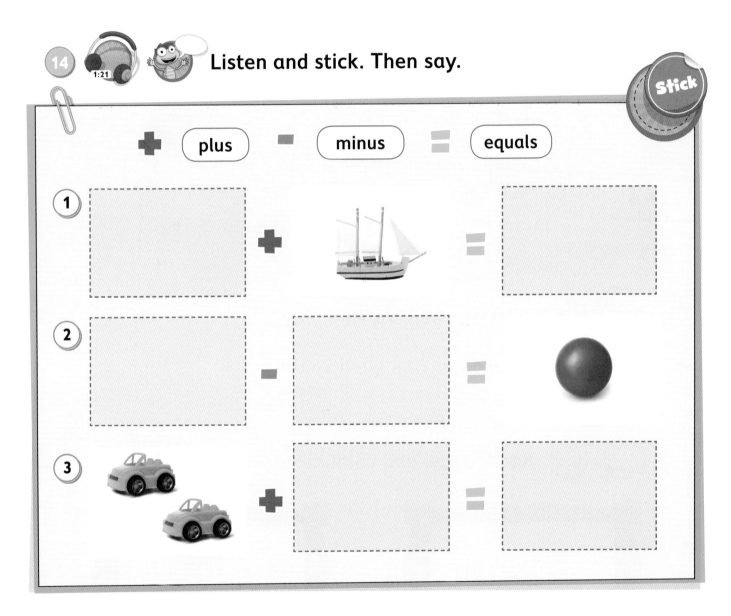

➕ plus ➖ minus ＝ equals

1

＋ ＝

2

➖ ＝

3

＋ ＝

PROJECT

15 Draw some sums for a friend.

16 **1:23** **Listen and number. Then trace.**

car

bike

ball

doll

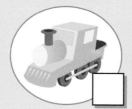

boat

train

kite

17   **1:24** **Listen. Then say and play.**

It's orange.

It's a ball.

18  **Read. Draw and colour.**

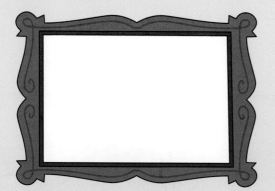

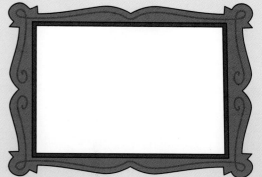

1 It's a kite. It's red.

2 twelve blue boats

19 **Listen. Then play.**

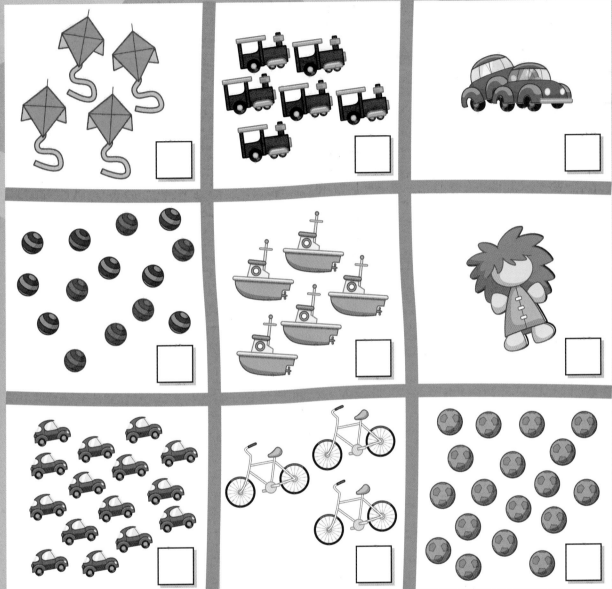

20 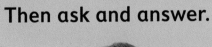 **Look at Activity 19. Count and write.**
Then ask and answer.

How many cars?

Two cars.

Now go to Poptropica
English World

2 My family

1 ⭐ **What do you know?**

granny

HELP WITH DINNER

grandad

cousin

2 🎧 1:26 Listen and circle.

3 🎧 1:27 Listen and say.

Can identify family members

4 Listen and chant.

friend

uncle

aunt

brother

sister

5 Listen and number. Then say.

a

b

c

d

Who's this?

She's my cousin.

 **6** **Listen and find. Then sing.**

bedroom

bathroom

living room

kitchen

 7  **Listen. Then say and play.**

She's in the living room.

Mum.

8 Play the game (page 73).

(page 73)

SPEAKING

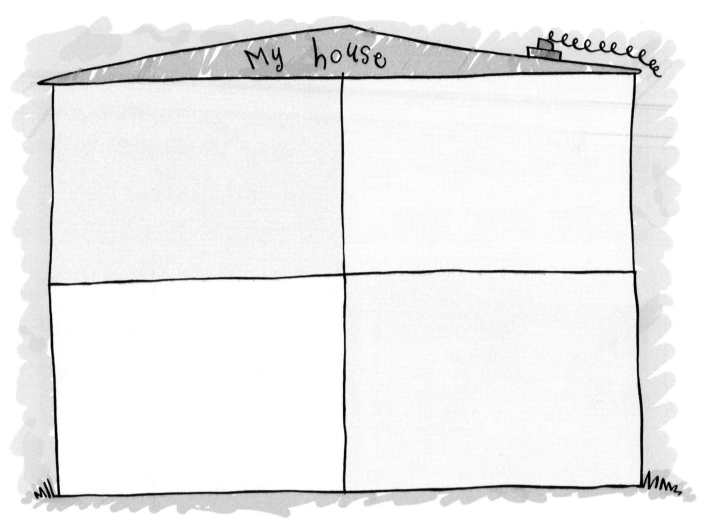
My house

SOUNDS FUN!

9 1:35 **Listen and say.**

Mum's on a bus with a bug.

Dad's in a van with a map.

11 **Act out the story.**

Can understand a simple story / Can act out a story

12 **1:39** **Listen and number.**

a | b | c | d

baby   young   old

13 **Look at Activity 12. Point and say.**

He's old.   She's young.

PROJECT

14 **Make a poster about your family.**
Tell the class about your poster.

old

This is my brother.
He's young.
This is my granny.
She's old.

young

Listen and stick. Then write.

| aunt | brother | grandad | granny | sisters | uncle |

Stick

1

2

_____

_____

3

4

_____

_____

Read and draw. Then say.

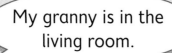

My granny is in the living room.

17 **Find and ✓.**

18 **Look at Activity 17. Ask and answer.**

Where's the aunt?

She's in the kitchen.

Now go to Poptropica English World

Lesson 8

Can use what I have learnt in Unit 2

19

3 My body

1 ⭐ **What do you know?**

fingers

hands

toes

legs

arms

2 🎧 1:41 **Listen and circle.**

3 🎧 1:42 **Listen and say.**

Can identify parts of the body

4 🎧 1:43 Listen and chant.

5 🎧 1:44 Listen and number.

6 1:46 / 1:47 **Listen and find. Then sing.**

 SONG

7 1:48 **Listen and ✓.**

HOME SCHOOL LINK

1

a

b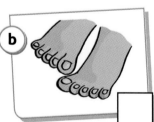

2

a

b

3

a

b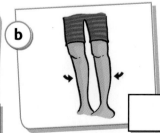

8   **Listen. Then play.**

I'm purple. I've got eight arms.

Number 2! Wave your arms.

9 **Listen and say.**

A big pink fish
with three green feet.

11 **Act out the story.**

12   1:56 **Listen and number. Then say.**

jump ☐   dance ☐   hop ☐

13 **Work in groups. Choose some actions for an exercise routine.**

 **a**	 **b**	 **c**	 **d**
Clap your hands.	Jump.	Stamp your feet.	Wave your arms.
 **e**	 **f**	 **g**	 **h**
Move your head.	Dance.	Touch your toes.	Shake your body.
 **i**	 **j**	 **k**	 **l**
Pull.	Push.	Hop.	Jump rope.

14  1:57 **Listen. Show the class your exercise routine.**

1	2	3	4	5	6

15 **Listen and stick. Then write.**

1.58

| arms | body | feet | hands | head | toes |

Stick

1 — Touch your _____.

2 — Move your _____.

3 — Stamp your _____.

4 — Wave your _____.

5 — Shake your _____.

6 — Clap your _____.

16 **Draw your body. Then say.**

I've got two...

I've got ten...

I've got one...

Can assess what I have learnt in Unit 3

17 **Choose and say. Then do.**

wave

touch

clap

move

shake

Touch your toes!

 18 **Play in pairs. Look and say.**

1  **2**  **3**  **4**  **5**

I've got six legs. I'm pink.

You're number 3.

Now go to Poptropica English World

4 My face

1 ⭐ What do you know?

hair

face

eyes

mouth

nose

ears

2 🎧 2:01 Listen and circle.

3 🎧 2:02 😄 Listen and say.

Can identify parts of the face

4 [2:03] 🎧 Listen and chant.

HELP THE DOCTOR

ARRIVALS

5 [2:04] 🎧 ✏️ Listen and draw. Then say.

I've got big eyes.

Lesson 2

Can talk about parts of the face using *have got*

29

Listen and find. Then sing.

7   **Listen and point. Then play.**

She's got a big nose.

Number 1.

1

2

3

4

Can describe faces / Can sing a song

8 **Make a face.**
Then play (page 75).

SOUNDS FUN!

9 2:10 **Listen and say.**

Old clothes for a big nose.   A baby plays with shapes.

1. Let's find the new doctor.

2. Has he got long hair?
No, he's got short hair.

3. He's got brown eyes.

4. Oh, no!
And he's got glasses.

5. Oops! Sorry!

6. Hello, I'm the new doctor.
Oh! Welcome to Tropical Island!

11   Act out the story.

Can understand a simple story / Can act out a story

12   **Listen and point. Then say.**

1
circle

2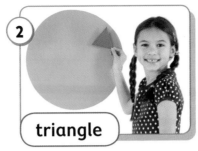
triangle

3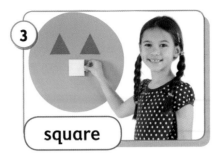
square

4
rectangle

5
It's a face.

PROJECT

13 **Draw and colour different shapes.**

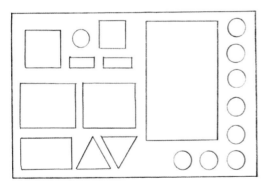 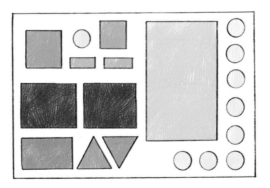

14 **Cut out the shapes. Make a shape picture.**

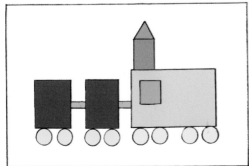

Lesson 6

Can describe shapes and make a shape picture   33

15  **Look and write. Then listen and say Emma or Tom.**

| ears | eyes | face | hair | mouth | nose |

a

1 _____

2 _____

3 _____

Emma

b

4 _____

5 _____

6 _____

Tom

16  **Draw a friend. Then write and say.**

| big | short | small | long |

This is _____.
(He's / She's) got _____
eyes and _____ hair.

Can assess what I have learnt in Unit 4

17 **Look and find. Circle ten differences.**

18  **Play in pairs. Look at Activity 17 and say.**

He's got glasses.

Picture 2.

Now go to Poptropica
English World

5 Animals

1 ⭐ What do you know?

sheep

horse

turkey

duck

2 🎧 **2:17** Listen and circle.

3 🎧 **2:18** Listen and say.

Can identify farm animals

4 2:19 Listen and chant.

cow

HELP THE FARMER

goat

hen

5 2:20 Listen and number.

a

b

c

d

Quest 2:21

Can understand descriptions of farm animals

37

Listen and find. Then sing.

frog

cat

dog

7 2:24 **Listen and ✓ or ✗. Then play.**

HOME SCHOOL LINK

1 2 3 4 5

Number two.
It's got four legs.

It's thin.

Yes!

No! It's fat.

Can describe animals / Can sing a song

8 **Play the game. Ask and answer.**  SPEAKING

It's got two legs.

Is it white? Is it a duck?

Yes!

SOUNDS FUN!

9  **Listen and say.**

A brown cow with a crown.   A short horse with a torch.

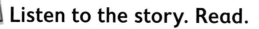

11   **Act out the story.**

Can understand a simple story / Can act out a story

12   **Listen and point. Then say.**

cow

1

duck

3

2

horse

4 bat

5 fox 6

owl

13   **Read and number.**

a It's brown.
It's awake
at night. ☐

b It's got big eyes.
It's awake
at night. ☐

c It's white.
It's awake in
the day. ☐

14  **Draw or find pictures of animals. Make a poster.**

15 Listen and stick. Then write.

cow   duck   goat   hen   horse   sheep   turkey

Stick

1   2   3   4

_____   _____   _____   _____

5   6   7

_____   _____   _____

16 Draw an animal. Then ask and answer.

Is it big?

Is it thin?

Can assess what I have learnt in Unit 5

17  **Circle the odd one out. Say.**

1

2

3

4

5

Now go to Poptropica English World

Lesson 8

Can use what I have learnt in Unit 5

6 Food

1 ⭐ **What do you know?**

rice

hot dogs

eggs

chicken

burgers

pizza

fish

bananas

apples

2 🎧 2:33 **Listen and circle.**

3 🎧 2:34 **Listen and say.**

Can identify food items

4 2:35 Listen and chant.

HELP WITH THE SHOPPING

5 2:36 Listen and number. Then say.

Quest 2:37

a

b

c

d

I like hot dogs.

salad

cheese

bread

RICE

7  **Listen and point. Then play.**

I like fish!

Number 1.

I don't like salad.

Number 4.

1

2

3

4

8 Play the game (page 77).

I like...

I don't like...

9 **Listen and say.**

SOUNDS FUN!

I like mice on bikes with white rice.

Listen to the story. Read.

 Act out the story.

48 **Lesson 5**

Can understand a simple story / Can act out a story

12   **Listen and circle.**
Then say.

SOCIAL SCIENCE

eggs

toast

cereal

bananas

breakfast

bread

apples

pizza

cheese

lunch

fish

rice

salad

chicken

dinner

PROJECT

13 **Draw or find pictures. Make a poster of your**
favourite meals.

Breakfast

Lunch

Dinner

Fish

Cereal

Hot dog

Rice

14   **Look and write. Then say.**

apple	banana	burger	chicken
egg	fish	hot dog	pizza	rice

1 **2** **3** **4** **5**

_____ _____ _____ _____ _____

6 **7** **8** **9**

_____ _____ _____ _____

15  **Draw two foods you like and don't like. Write.**

I like _____   I don't like _____
and _____.   or _____.

16 **Look at Activity 15. Say with a partner.**

I like bananas.

I don't like burgers.

Can assess what I have learnt in Unit 6

17 **Play the game.**

 HAVE FUN

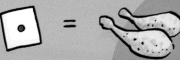 =  = =

 =  = =

Number 2. Hot dogs.

a
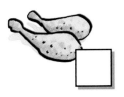 

b
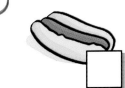 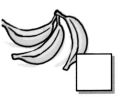

c
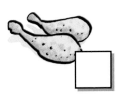 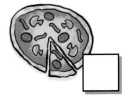

d

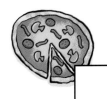 

Now go to Poptropica
English World

Lesson 8

Can use what I have learnt in Unit 6

7 Clothes

1 ⭐ **What do you know?**

HELP
WITH THE
CLOTHES

dress

skirt

shoes

2 🎧 3:01 **Listen and circle.**

3 🎧 3:02 **Listen and say.**

Can identify clothes

4 🎧 3:03 Listen and chant.

hat

T-shirt

trousers

socks

5 🎧 3:04 ✏️ Listen and colour. Then say.

1

2

3

Quest 3:05

I'm wearing a yellow dress.

Lesson 2

Can describe what I'm wearing

53

Listen and find. Then sing.

① pyjamas

②

③ jumper

④ boots

  Listen. Then play.

Take off your shoes.

Number 3!

 ①

 ②

 ③

 ④

SPEAKING

8   **Listen. Then colour and say.**

I'm a boy. I'm wearing a blue jumper. I'm wearing red trousers.

● red ● orange ● yellow
● blue ● green ● purple

SOUNDS FUN!

9   **Listen and say.**

A nurse with a skirt and a purple bird.

1

Where's my hat?
Have you got my hat?

2

I'm wearing trousers.
Where's my dress?

And where's
my HAT?

3

Is your dress pink?

No! My dress is blue!

4

Nice
dress!

Oh! Thank you!

Where's my hat, PLEASE?

5

Ooh!
Nice hats!

6

Thank you.
This is for you.

Thank
you!

11   Act out the story.

Can understand a simple story / Can act out a story

7

12   **Listen and read. Then say.**

I'm a firefighter. I'm wearing a helmet.

I'm a chef. I'm wearing a white hat.

I'm a nurse. I'm wearing a blue dress.

I'm a police officer. I'm wearing a white shirt.

1 firefighter

2 chef

3 nurse

4

police officer

PROJECT

13   **Draw a picture of someone wearing a uniform.**

Make a poster about a uniform.

I'm a Police Officer.

I'm wearing a white shirt.

I'm wearing blue trousers.

I'm wearing black shoes.

14 **Listen and stick. Then write.**

| dress | hat | shoes | skirt | socks | trousers | T-shirt |

Stick

_____ _____ _____

_____ _____ _____ _____

15   **Draw and colour your clothes. Then write.**

I'm wearing _____

_____

_____ .

16   **Listen and find. Then say.**

1  2  3  4

 I'm wearing a yellow dress, blue shoes, white socks and a pink hat.

Now go to Poptropica
English World

Lesson 8 Can use what I have learnt in Unit 7 **59**

8 Weather

snowy

 1 ⭐ **What do you know?**

cloudy

sunny

HELP AT THE MOUNTAIN

windy

 2 🎧 3:19 **Listen and circle.**

 **3** 🎧 3:20 😃 **Listen and say.**

60 **Lesson 1**

Can identify types of weather

4 🎧 3:21 **Listen and chant.**

rainy

cool

5 🎧 3:22 ✏️ **Listen and draw. Then say.**

1

2

3

4

Quest
3:23

6   **Listen and find. Then sing.**

7   **Listen and point. Then play.**

It's a sunny day.

It's Picture 1.

Can talk about the weather / Can sing a song

8   Listen. Then play (page 79).

Do you like sunny days?

Yes.

snowy days ☐

bananas ☐

horses ☐

sunny days ☐

salad ☐

dolls ☐

pink dresses ☐

dogs ☐

cars ☐

SOUNDS FUN!

9  Listen and say.

A moose with blue boots on a scooter.

11   **Act out the story.**

12   Listen and say.

Monday **Tuesday** **Wednesday**
Thursday **Friday** **Saturday** **Sunday**

13 Draw pictures of the weather.

14  Make a weather chart. Write the days of the week.

Monday	Tuesday	Wednesday	Thursday	Friday
Sunny	Cloudy	Windy		

15 Listen and stick. Then write.

cloudy   rainy   snowy   sunny   windy

1 Monday

It's _____.

2 Tuesday

It's _____.

3 Wednesday

It's _____.

4 Thursday

It's _____.

5 Friday

It's _____.

16 Draw yourself on your favourite day. Then write.

It's _____.

It's _____.

I like _____ days.

I don't like _____ days.

17 Now say.

Do you like sunny days?

No. I like snowy days.

Can assess what I have learnt in Unit 8

18   **Listen and follow. Then say.**

19 **Listen and act.**

Now go to Poptropica
English World

Goodbye

1 🎧 3:37 Listen and circle.

glasses

bananas

doctor

2 🎧 3:38 Listen and number.

a

b

c

d

e

f

g

h

Can identify food

3 Quest song. Listen and sing.

sun

pizza

hair

dress

4 Draw five of your favourite things. Then show and tell.

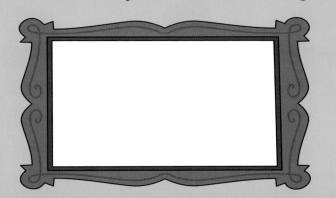

Goodbye!

Christmas

1   Listen and sing. Then find and say.

star

Christmas tree

stocking

presents

Santa

2 Make. Then give and say.

Happy Christmas!

Can talk about Christmas / Can make a Christmas present

Valentine's Day

   Listen and sing. Then find and say.

flowers

heart

card

chocolates

2 **Make and play.**

Two hearts!

Easter

1 **Make. Then listen and sing.**

2 **Play the game.**

rabbit

	1		2	
egg	1		1	
chick	2		2	
flower	3		3	

Can talk about Easter / Can play an Easter game

Cutouts. Unit 2, Lesson 4, Page 15.

Name: _____

Name: _____

Name: _____

Name: _____

Name: _____

Name: _____

Name: _____
_____

Name: _____
_____

Name: _____
_____

Name: _____
_____

Cutouts. Unit 4, Lesson 4, Page 31.

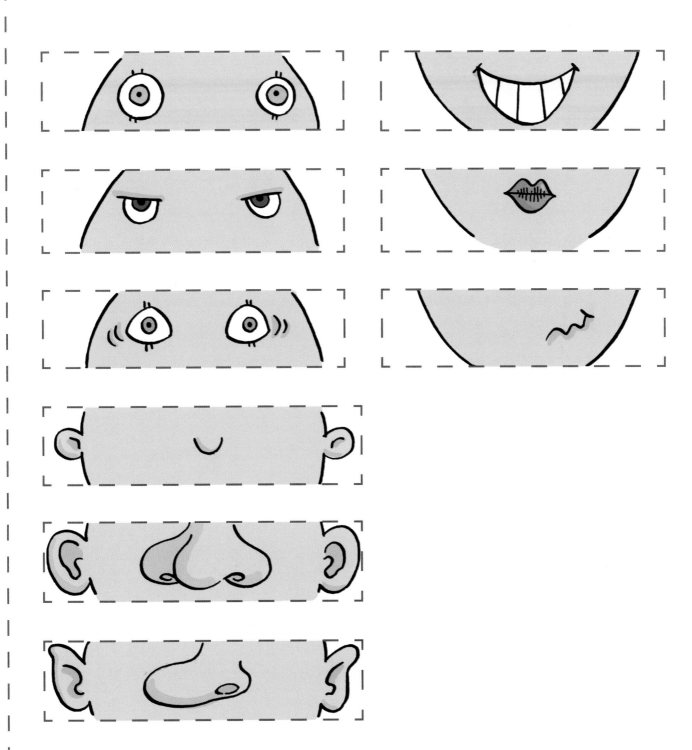

Name: _____

Name: _____

Name: _____

Name: _____

Name: _____

Name: _____

Name: _____

Name: _____

Cutouts. Unit 6, Lesson 4, Page 47.

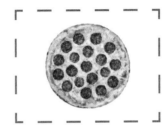

Cutouts. Unit 8, Lesson 4, Page 63.

Name:_____

Name:_____

Name:_____

Name:_____

Name:_____

Name:_____

Name:_____

Name:_____

Name:_____